Body Coverings

Shells

Cassie Mayer

Heinemann
LIBRARY

H www.heinemann.co.uk/library

Visit our website to find out more information about **Heinemann Library** books.

To order:
☎ Phone 44 (0) 1865 888066
▤ Send a fax to 44 (0) 1865 314091
▯ Visit the Heinemann Bookshop at www.heinemann.co.uk/library to browse our catalogue and order online.

First published in Great Britain by Heinemann Library, Halley Court, Jordan Hill, Oxford OX2 8EJ, part of Harcourt Education. Heinemann is a registered trademark of Harcourt Education Ltd.

© Harcourt Education Ltd 2006.
First published in paperback in 2007.
The moral right of the proprietor has been asserted.

Editorial: Tracey Crawford, Cassie Mayer, Dan Nunn, and Sarah Chappelow
Design: Jo Hinton-Malivoire
Picture Research: Tracy Cummins
Production: Duncan Gilbert

Originated by Chroma Graphics (Overseas) Pte. Ltd
Printed and bound in China by South China Printing Company

13 digit ISBN 978 0 431 18278 0 (hardback)

11 10 09 08 07 06
10 9 8 7 6 5 4 3 2 1

13 digit ISBN 978 0 431 18284 1 (paperback)

11 10 09 08 07
10 9 8 7 6 5 4 3 2 1

British Library Cataloguing in Publication Data
Mayer, Cassie
  Shells. – (Body coverings)
  1.Shells – Juvenile literature
  I.Title
  591.4'77

Acknowledgements
The publishers would like to thank the following for permission to reproduce photographs:
Corbis pp. **6** (Martin Harvey), **7** and **8** (Jeffrey L. Rotman), **13** and **14** (Sally A. Morgan/Ecoscene), **15** and **16** (Brownie Harris), **20** (Kevin Dodge), **22** (oyster, Louie Psihoyos); Getty Images/Digital Vision p. **4** (kingfisher, leopard, rhino); Getty Images/PhotoDisc pp. **4** (lizard), **5**, **23** (snail); Nature Picture Library pp. **11** (Jurgen Freund), **12** (Jurgen Freund), **17** (Pete Oxford), **18** (Pete Oxford), **23** (tortoise, Pete Oxford); Seapics pp. **9**, **10**, **22** (horse shoe crab and hermit crab).

Cover photograph of shells, reproduced with permission of Getty Images/Brand X Pictures. Back cover image of crab reproduced with permission of Seapics.

Special thanks to the Smithsonian Institution and Gary E. Davis for their help with this project.

Every effort has been made to contact copyright holders of any material reproduced in this book. Any omissions will be rectified in subsequent printings if notice is given to the publishers.

The paper used to print this book comes from sustainable resources.

Contents

Body coverings 4

Types of shell 6

Shell quiz 21

Fun shell facts 22

Picture glossary 23

Index 24

Notes 24

feathers

fur

scales

skin

All animals have body coverings.
Look at these body coverings.

shell

Some animals have shells.
Shells are a body covering too.

There are many types of shell.
Some animals find shells to live in.

Shells can be smooth.
What animal is this?

shell

cowrie

This animal is a cowrie.
It has a shiny shell.

Shells can be rough.
What animal is this?

This animal is a crab.
Its shell has bumps.

Shells can be big.
What animal is this?

This animal is a giant clam.
It can open and close its shell.

Shells can be small.
What animal is this?

barnacle

This animal is a barnacle.
It clings to rocks and wood.

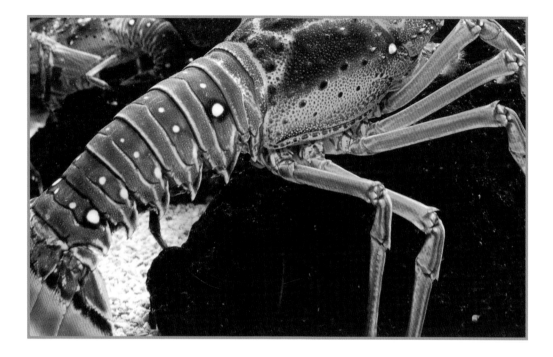

Shells can be bright colours.
What animal is this?

This animal is a lobster.
Its shell is in segments so it can bend.

Shells can have patterns.
What animal is this?

This animal is a tortoise.
The patterns on its shell help it to hide.

Do you have a shell?

No! You do not have a shell!
You have skin.

Shell quiz

(answers on page 24)

1. I live in the sea.
   I run sideways.
   I have a rough shell.
   What am I?

2. I have four legs.
   I move slowly.
   I have a patterned shell.
   What am I?

Fun shell facts

Horse shoe crabs have been on the Earth for millions of years.

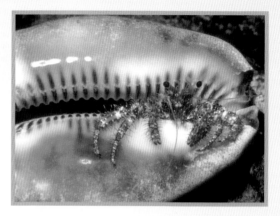

Hermit crabs find shells to hide in.

Oysters create pearls. Pearls are used to make jewellery.

Picture glossary

pattern an arrangement of markings. Patterns help some animals hide.

shell a type of body covering. Many animals with shells live in the sea.

Index

body covering
4, 5
barnacle 13, 14
cowrie 9, 10

crab 9, 10, 22
giant clam 11, 12
lobster 15, 16
tortoise 17, 18

Notes to parents and teachers

Before reading
Talk about how animals have different body coverings – shells, fur, feathers, scales, and skin. Talk about the different kinds of shells – some shells are smooth (snail), some shells are rough (crab), some shells are big (giant clam), and some shells are small (barnacle). Explain that some creatures with shells have a soft body (e.g. snails and tortoises). When they are moving or feeding, their soft bodies come out from their shells but if there is danger they can hide inside their shells. Crabs have a hard shell covering all over their bodies. Hermit crabs use other shells to hide in.

After reading
Collect pictures of animals with different shells from catalogues and magazines. Ask the children to sort them into categories e.g. big, small, rough, smooth. Teach the children the following tongue-twister:
She sells sea shells on the sea shore.
The shells that she sells are sea shells I'm sure.

Answers to quiz: 1. I am a crab. 2. I am a tortoise.